Read-About® Geography

WITHDRAWN

Nevada

By Susan Labella

Subject Consultant
Herb Thomas
Co-Coordinator
Geographic Alliance In Nevada
Reno, Nevada

Reading Consultant
Cecilia Minden-Cupp, PhD
Former Director of the Language and Literacy Program
Harvard Graduate School of Education
Cambridge, Massachusetts

Children's Press®
A Division of Scholastic Inc.
New York   Toronto   London   Auckland   Sydney
Mexico City   New Delhi   Hong Kong
Danbury, Connecticut

Designer: Herman Adler
Photo Researcher: Caroline Anderson
The photo on the cover shows rock formations and cliffs in Nevada's Valley of Fire.

Library of Congress Cataloging-in-Publication Data

Labella, Susan, 1948–
  Nevada / by Susan Labella.
      p. cm. — (Rookie read-about geography)
  Includes index.
  ISBN 13: 978-0-516-25467-8 (lib. bdg.)   978-0-531-16815-8 (pbk.)
  ISBN 10: 0-516-25467-7 (lib. bdg.)   0-531-16815-8 (pbk.)
  1. Nevada—Juvenile literature. 2. Nevada—Geography—Juvenile
literature. I. Title. II. Series.
  F841.3.L33 2007
  979.3—dc22   2006004592

CHILDREN'S PRESS, and ROOKIE READ-ABOUT®, and associated
logos are trademarks and/or registered trademarks of Scholastic Library
Publishing. SCHOLASTIC and associated logos are trademarks and/or
registered trademarks of Scholastic Inc.
1 2 3 4 5 6 7 8 9 10 R 16 15 14 13 12 11 10 09 08 07

Desert sagebrush

Which state is called the Sagebrush State?

It's Nevada!

Nevada is in the western part of the United States. Can you find Nevada on this map?

CANADA

WASHINGTON
OREGON
IDAHO
MONTANA
NORTH DAKOTA
SOUTH DAKOTA
WYOMING
NEVADA
UTAH
CALIFORNIA
ARIZONA
COLORADO
NEW MEXICO
MINNESOTA
WISCONSIN
MICHIGAN
NEBRASKA
IOWA
ILLINOIS
INDIANA
KANSAS
MISSOURI
OKLAHOMA
ARKANSAS
TEXAS
LOUISIANA
MISSISSIPPI
ALABAMA
TENNESSEE
KENTUCKY
OHIO
WEST VIRGINIA
VIRGINIA
NORTH CAROLINA
SOUTH CAROLINA
GEORGIA
FLORIDA
NEW HAMPSHIRE
VERMONT
MAINE
NEW YORK
PENNSYLVANIA
MASSACHUSETTS
RHODE ISLAND
CONNECTICUT
NEW JERSEY
DELAWARE
MARYLAND
Washington, D.C.

North
West   East
South

ALASKA   CANADA

MEXICO

HAWAII

5

Sagebrush

The hot Mojave (mo-HAH-vee) Desert stretches across southern Nevada.

Sagebrush grows in this area. Sagebrush is a short, woody plant. It is Nevada's state flower.

You'll see more than sagebrush in Nevada's desert. If you are lucky, you might spot a desert tortoise.

These tortoises live in underground burrows, or holes. The burrows keep tortoises safe from the hot desert sun.

A desert tortoise

Visitors hiking through a Nevada canyon

Nevada has many mountains, too. These are perfect for skiing and hiking.

The highest point in Nevada is Boundary Peak in the White Mountains. It rises more than 13,000 feet (4,000 meters).

Boundary Peak

A bristlecone pine

Forests of bristlecone pine trees grow in Nevada's Great Basin National Park. Some of these trees are thousands of years old!

The bristlecone pine is
one of Nevada's state trees.
Nevada's other state tree is
the single-leaf pinon pine.

A single-leaf pinon pine

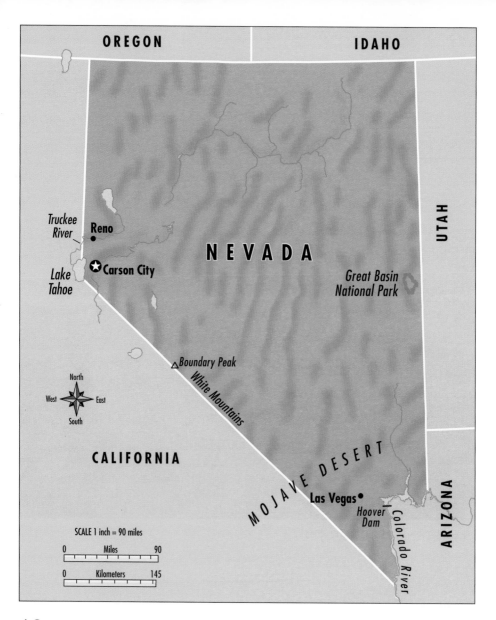

OREGON

IDAHO

UTAH

Truckee
River

Reno

Lake
Tahoe

Carson City

NEVADA

Great Basin
National Park

△ Boundary Peak

White Mountains

North

West ✦ East

South

CALIFORNIA

M O J A V E   D E S E R T

Las Vegas ●

Hoover
Dam

Colorado River

ARIZONA

SCALE 1 inch = 90 miles

| 0 | Miles | 90 |

| 0 | Kilometers | 145 |

The capital of Nevada
is Carson City.

Carson City is home
to several museums,
including a railroad
museum and a
children's museum.

Lake Tahoe is near Carson City. Visitors to Lake Tahoe can boat, fish, swim, or even ride in a hot-air balloon.

Tour boats on Lake Tahoe

Reno's River Walk

Reno is in western Nevada. The Truckee River flows through downtown Reno.

Some people bike along the River Walk. Others enjoy visiting the area's many small shops.

Hoover Dam is located on the border of Nevada and Arizona.

A dam is used to hold back water. Hoover Dam was built in the 1930s to stop the Colorado River from flooding.

Hoover Dam

Downtown Las Vegas

26

Las Vegas is in southern Nevada. It is Nevada's largest city.

Las Vegas has fancy hotels, bright lights, and fun shows for you to see.

There is so much to see
and do in Nevada.

What will you do first
when you get there?

A visitor to Nevada fishes in a local lake.

Words You Know

Boundary Peak

desert tortoise

Hoover Dam

Lake Tahoe

30

Las Vegas

Reno

sagebrush

single-leaf pinon pine

Index

animals, 8

ballooning, 20

boating, 20

Boundary Peak, 12

bristlecone pine trees, 15, 16

Carson City, 19

cities, 19, 23, 27

Colorado River, 24

dams, 24

desert tortoises, 8

deserts, 7

fishing, 20

forests, 15

Great Basin National Park, 15

hiking, 11

Hoover Dam, 24

Lake Tahoe, 20

Las Vegas, 27

Mojave Desert, 7

mountains, 11, 12

museums, 19

plants, 7

Reno, 23

River Walk, 23

sagebrush, 7

single-leaf pinon pine trees, 16

skiing, 11

state capital, 19

state flower, 7

state nickname, 3

state trees, 16

swimming, 20

trees, 15, 16

Truckee River, 23

White Mountains, 12

About the Author

Susan Labella is a former teacher and editor. She is currently a freelance writer and has written other books in the Rookie Read-About® Geography series.

Photo Credits

Photographs © 2007: Alamy Images/Thomas Hallstein: 10; Corbis Images: 26, 31 top left (Robert Essel, NYC), 25, 30 bottom left (Blaine Harrington III), 13, 30 top left (Galen Rowell), 29 (Royalty-Free); Getty Images/Richard Olsenius/ National Geographic: 14; Index Stock Imagery/James Denk: cover; John Elk III: 3, 6, 22, 31 top right, 31 bottom left; Minden Pictures/Larry Minden; 9, 30 top right; ShutterStock, Inc./Mike Norton: 21, 30 bottom right; Visuals Unlimited/ Doug Sokell: 17, 31 bottom right.

Maps by Bob Italiano